# Lacy Sunshine
# Rory's Seasons Coloring Book

MW01204309

## Illustrated by Artist Heather Valentin
### Volume 39

This book belongs
to

_____

# Sneak Peek

Upcoming Lacy Sunshine Coloring Books

Fairy Lanterns and Fairy Doors

Enjoy, Heather

97057919R00033